EXPLORING THE
CHESAPEAKE BAY

VISITING
THE CHESAPEAKE BAY

By Kathleen Connors

Gareth Stevens
Publishing

Please visit our website, www.garethstevens.com. For a free color catalog of all our high-quality books, call toll free 1-800-542-2595 or fax 1-877-542-2596.

Library of Congress Cataloging-in-Publication Data

Connors, Kathleen.
Visiting the Chesapeake Bay / by Kathleen Connors.
  p. cm. — (Exploring the Chesapeake Bay)
Includes index.
ISBN 978-1-4339-9789-1 (pbk.)
ISBN 978-1-4339-9790-7 (6-pack)
ISBN 978-1-4339-9788-4 (library binding)
1. Chesapeake Bay (Md. and Va.)—Juvenile literature. 2. Chesapeake Bay (Md. and Va.)—
Geography—Juvenile literature. I. Connors, Kathleen. II. Title.
F187.C5 C66 2014
975.2—d23

First Edition

Published in 2014 by
Gareth Stevens Publishing
111 East 14th Street, Suite 349
New York, NY 10003

Copyright © 2014 Gareth Stevens Publishing

Designer: Andrea Davison-Bartolotta
Editor: Kristen Rajczak

Photo credits: Cover, p.1 Eastwoods Photos/Shutterstock.com; pp. 4–5 Hulton Archive/
Getty Images; pp. 4 (map), 29 (map) Globe Turner/Shutterstock.com; pp. 6–7 Rich Clement/
Bloomberg via Getty Images; p. 9 (map) courtesy of Chesapeake Bay Program; p. 9
(background) Jon Beard/Shutterstock.com; p. 10 Stephen St. John/National Geographic/
Getty Images; pp. 10–11 Eileen McVey/NOAA; p. 13 Skip Brown/National Geographic/Getty
Images; p. 14 courtesy of NOAA; p. 15 Michael S. Williamson/The Wahington Post via Getty
Images; p. 17 Greg Pease/Photographer's Choice/Getty Images; p. 19 courtesy of US Navy;
p. 20 (left inset) aceshot1/Shutterstock.com; p. 20 (right inset) Ken Schulze/Shutterstock.com;
pp. 20–21 (background), 27 (inset), 28–29 (background) iStockphoto/Thinkstock; p. 21 (inset)
Gordon Schmidt/Flickr/Getty Images; p. 23 Glynnis Jones/Shutterstock.com; pp. 24–25
Cameron Davidson/Photographer's Choice/Getty Images; p. 26 Jerry Driendl/Getty Images;
p. 27 (main) Paul Souders/Stone/Getty Images.

Printed in the United States of America

CPSIA compliance information: Batch #CS13GS: For further information contact Gareth Stevens, New York, New York at 1-800-542-2595.

CONTENTS

Words in the glossary appear in **bold** type the first time they are used in the text.

LEAD THE WAY TO THE BAY

In 1607, England established its first permanent colony in North America. The Jamestown Colony was settled on a **peninsula** in the James River—right off the Chesapeake Bay. The settlement grew for almost 150 years before the 13 colonies declared independence from England. And some of that success can be credited to the excellent location of the Chesapeake Bay, as well as the abundance of resources available there.

Today, the population of the Chesapeake Bay region grows every year. The bay serves as a gateway to the active ports of the Atlantic coast, and the region is a popular vacation spot.

MD.

Anna

Chesapeake Bay

Jamestown

ATLANTIC OCEAN

NOT EXACTLY PERFECT

Though it was in a great location for receiving ships, the Jamestown Colony had problems being settled right near the Chesapeake Bay. The wetlands and **humidity** caused frequent illness among the colonists. Trouble with nearby Native Americans caused the original settlers to try to leave after just a few years, too! By 1614, however, a more peaceful relationship had been forged, and the colonists began to grow a very profitable crop—tobacco.

The Jamestown Colony was settled near present-day Williamsburg, Virginia.

The Chesapeake Bay is found between Maryland and Virginia. Delaware, New York, Pennsylvania, West Virginia, and Washington, DC, are part of the bay's 64,000-square-mile (165,760 sq km) **watershed**, as well.

Two of the biggest US ports on the Atlantic coast—Baltimore, Maryland, and Hampton Roads, Virginia—are found on the Chesapeake Bay. In addition, about 500 million pounds (227 million kg) of seafood are harvested from the bay each year!

Tobacco remains an export, though manufacturing has become somewhat more important than agriculture. The military can be considered a key industry in the bay area, too, with both the US Naval Academy and Naval Station Norfolk nearby.

From the first settlement of the Chesapeake Bay region to today, the bay has been an important port for both military and economic uses.

Port of Baltimore USA

MAJOR CITIES OF THE CHESAPEAKE BAY

city	state	population (2010 census)
Baltimore	Maryland	620,961
Norfolk	Virginia	242,803
Newport News	Virginia	180,719
Hampton	Virginia	137,436
Portsmouth	Virginia	95,535
Annapolis	Maryland	38,394

THE NATURAL BAY

The Chesapeake Bay region offers much to visitors interested in nature. First, there's the bay itself: it's an estuary! An estuary is a body of water where salt water and freshwater meet and mix. That makes the bay a **unique** place to see plants and animals. Some, such as the famous blue crab, live part of their life in the freshwater of the bay's **tributaries** and part in the saltier waters that come in from the Atlantic Ocean.

The largest rivers that bring freshwater into the Chesapeake Bay are the Susquehanna, the Potomac, and the James Rivers. About 150 streams, rivers, and creeks flow into the bay in total.

A HISTORIC RIVER

A lot of US history has taken place on the shores of the Potomac River. George Washington's home, Mount Vernon, is along the Potomac. In 1859, a slave uprising at Harpers Ferry occurred on the river. During the **American Civil War**, the Battle of Antietam was fought close to the Potomac, too. Today, you can visit all these places to learn more about them!

NY

PA

Susquehanna River

WV

MD

Chester River

Washington, DC

Choptank River

DE

Patuxent River

Potomac River

Nanticoke River

VA

Rappahannock River

Wicomico River

York River

Chesapeake Bay

James River

This map shows many of the major rivers that are part of the Chesapeake Bay watershed.

One way to experience the natural and historic region of the Chesapeake Bay is through national parks. The Captain John Smith National Historic Trail marks the water routes John Smith took when he mapped the bay area from 1607 to 1609. It's part of the Chesapeake Bay Gateways Network, a series of water trails, hiking paths, and historic sites in Maryland, Virginia, Delaware, and Washington, DC.

Piscataway Park in Accokeek, Maryland, has forests and wetlands as well as a fishing pier for visitors to enjoy. It's right on the Potomac River and offers a great view of Mount Vernon, too!

SANDY POINT STATE PARK, MARYLAND

PROTECTING AND SAVING THE BAY

The **ecosystem** of the Chesapeake Bay has many problems. Pollution and poor water quality trouble plants and animals alike. Many sea creatures are overharvested. Groups dedicated to the bay's cause work hard to get laws passed and land set aside to keep the bay safe. But **conservation** efforts are still necessary.

The many national parks in the Chesapeake Bay region offer opportunities to view beautiful wildlife.

HOW'S THE WEATHER?

The nearness of the Atlantic Ocean and the Chesapeake Bay greatly impact the climate of the cities on the bay. They help to moderate the weather and make the region a pleasant place to live most of the year.

Both southeastern Maryland and eastern Virginia have a humid, subtropical climate. During the summer, humidity can be very high—nearing 100 percent—because of the water in the air from the ocean and the bay. It may also reach 100°F (38°C)! In January, the average temperature is between 35°F and 40°F (2°C and 4°C).

STICKY SUMMERS

If you're visiting the Chesapeake Bay area during the summer, you might have a beautiful, sunny day—but it could be awfully "sticky" from the humidity, and it can be hot. In 2011, temperatures in Baltimore one day reached 108°F (42°C)! In the next few decades, scientists think these high temperatures could be more frequent. The water temperature will also rise, causing problems for the plants and animals that live there. Some may even die out.

The generally warm climate of the Chesapeake Bay region is one of the reasons so many people vacation there.

GROWTH ISN'T ALWAYS GOOD

More than 17 million people live in the Chesapeake Bay watershed, and that number continues to grow. It's been said that this population growth works against conservation efforts. More people means that more homes need to be built, harming the **habitats** of bay plants and animals. Industries like farming and logging create pollution that ends up in the bay.

Nonetheless, the bay's natural beauty, mild climate, and economic possibilities are a major draw to Americans and **immigrants** alike. The next several pages will introduce some of the major cities that have emerged near the Chesapeake Bay, and what each has come to offer.

VOLUNTEERS WORK TO CLEAN UP THE PATUXENT RIVER

HOME FOR ALL KINDS

Not only are there millions of people living in and around the Chesapeake Bay, but there are also thousands of plants and animals. Almost 30 kinds of waterfowl and about 350 kinds of fish make their homes in the many habitats of the bay. They live among the underwater grasses, in shallow waters of the tributaries, on sandy beaches, and on the bay's muddy bottom.

Sailing, fishing, and taking nature hikes are just some of the fun activities to take advantage of when near the Chesapeake Bay.

CHARM CITY

Baltimore is the largest city in Maryland. It's found at the head of the Patapsco River, about 15 miles (24 km) from the Chesapeake Bay. One of the major US ports on the Atlantic coast, Baltimore is known for making and shipping cars, as well as manufacturing steel, electronics, and airplane parts. There's also a lot for visitors to do there!

Did you know Babe Ruth was born in Baltimore? Near the city's famous inner harbor, the Babe Ruth Birthplace and Museum exhibits his uniforms, bats, and photos of his baseball triumphs. The grave of poet Edgar Allan Poe is also in Baltimore! He was born there, too.

THE BOMBS BURSTING IN AIR

"The Star-Spangled Banner" celebrates a battle that occurred at Fort McHenry, right outside Baltimore! During the War of 1812, the British tried to take Baltimore—but the forces at Fort McHenry kept them back. Today, the fort is a national monument at the mouth of the Baltimore Harbor.

See the historic USS *Constellation* in Baltimore's inner harbor. You can even walk on its decks!

17

HAMPTON ROADS

The second large port in the Chesapeake Bay area is Hampton Roads, Virginia. Hampton Roads is a roadstead formed by the James River. A roadstead is a harbor-like place where ships can anchor. Hampton Roads includes the cities facing the port, such as Hampton, Norfolk, Virginia Beach, and Newport News.

Though the Port of Hampton Roads is a leading shipping location, it's perhaps best known as a military center. The Norfolk Naval Shipyard is the oldest in the country. There are air force, marines, and coast guard activities there, too. Langley Air Force Base near Hampton is the headquarters of the 1st Fighter Wing and Air Combat Command, among others.

HISTORY AT THE ROADS

The Port of Hampton Roads is one of the busiest US ports in use today—and it's been active since the early days of the United States. The naval battle between the ships *Monitor* and *Merrimac* took place at Hampton Roads during the American Civil War. A few years later, it was the place Abraham Lincoln met with Southern leaders for peace talks.

The USS *Harry S. Truman*, an aircraft carrier, travels from the Norfolk Naval Shipyard on the Elizabeth River.

Norfolk, Virginia Beach, and Newport News are popular vacation spots! In fact, Virginia Beach began as a resort town as far back as the 1880s. Today, many hotels line the shores of Virginia Beach and overlook miles of ocean beaches. Back Bay National Wildlife Refuge offers a completely different experience. There, 9,250 acres (3,746 ha) of land have been set aside to preserve natural marshes, beaches, and woodlands. Visitors can follow hiking trails and try to spot loggerhead turtles and bald eagles!

The Virginia Zoo in Norfolk offers another place to see wild animals. Its conservation projects help the animals living in the Chesapeake Bay, such as oysters.

VIRGINIA BEACH

BACK BAY NATIONAL WILDLIFE REFUGE

PASSPORT TO THE PAST

LIGHTHOUSE AT CAPE HENRY IN VIRGINIA

Only 6 miles (9.7 km) from Virginia Beach is Cape Henry. It's right on the entrance to the Chesapeake Bay. A memorial stands there today marking the place where the Jamestown colonists first landed in 1607! The Mariners' Museum in Newport News is the largest **maritime** museum in North America. Visitors can learn more about the Chesapeake Bay and famous ships there.

From Virginia Beach, pictured here, visitors can easily travel to historic sites like Yorktown and Colonial Williamsburg.

ANNAPOLIS

Though small in size and population, Annapolis, Maryland, has long been an important city on the Chesapeake Bay. Located where the Severn River opens into the bay, Annapolis has been the capital city of Maryland since 1694.

Annapolis's Colonial Historic District is 40 city blocks! It has more buildings constructed before the **American Revolution** than any district in the United States. The houses of three men who signed the Declaration of Independence still stand there!

In addition to history, Annapolis hosts big boat shows and is a great place for those who sail. Cruises around the Chesapeake Bay often leave from docks in Annapolis.

ANNAPOLIS FACTS

Founded: 1649

First names: Providence, Town Land at Proctor's, Anne Arundel Town

Landmarks: US Naval Academy, Maryland State House

Famous natives: New England Patriots' head coach Bill Belichick; author Barbara Kingsolver

Did You Know? Colonists in Annapolis also had a "tea party" in 1774 to protest the British tax on tea.

The Maryland State House is the oldest legislative building used today. The Treaty of Paris, which ended the American Revolution, was approved by Congress there!

THE CHESAPEAKE BAY BRIDGE-TUNNEL

Since 1964, the Chesapeake Bay Bridge-Tunnel has allowed easier travel through the region. It's also become a major landmark and must-see attraction for tourists.

The roadway is 17.6 miles (28.3 km) long from shore to shore, crossing the bay to connect the Hampton Roads area with Cape Charles.

Some of the best views of the Chesapeake Bay can be found when driving along the bridge-tunnel, officially named the Lucius J. Kellam Jr. Bridge-Tunnel in 1987.

The bridges are quite a sight themselves, with four man-made islands connecting them and nothing but the Atlantic Ocean beyond! But what about the tunnel parts? Cars and trucks are driving underneath the Chesapeake Bay! The tunnels allow for more traffic without taking up valuable shipping lanes in the water.

FERRY ME HOME

Before the bridge-tunnel was built, boats called ferries carried passengers from the northeastern shore of Virginia across the Chesapeake Bay. As travel needs increased in the 1950s, the Chesapeake Bay Ferry Commission looked into building a driving route. Similarly, travel needs were growing in 1990 when a parallel crossing project was proposed. A new part of the bay bridge-tunnel opened in 1999.

VISIT THE CHESAPEAKE BAY

Do you want to explore the Chesapeake Bay? There are so many natural and historic places to visit, it might seem impossible to see them all! If your interests lie elsewhere, there's still plenty to do. Catch a Baltimore Orioles baseball game at the famous Camden Yards. Built in 1992, it's meant to look like a ballpark from the 1920s!

A seafood feast might be on the menu when you visit the Chesapeake Bay! Crisfield, Maryland, found on the bay's eastern shore, is called the "crab capital of the world." From oysters to shrimp, restaurants around the Chesapeake Bay offer some of the freshest, tastiest seafood around.

CAMDEN YARDS

DON'T MISS DC

It's only about an hour's drive from Baltimore to Washington, DC, making a tour of our nation's capital an easy addition to a trip to the Chesapeake Bay. The National Archives Building houses the original Declaration of Independence, while the Smithsonian's National Museum of American History has other historic items—like the ruby slippers from *The Wizard of Oz*!

CRAB CAKES

Head to Crisfield to enjoy a big basket of crabs for dinner!

CITIES OF THE CHESAPEAKE BAY

With its abundance of natural resources and access to many waterways, the Chesapeake Bay has been a population center since the founding of the United States. Check out where the major cities are using this map!

FAST CITY FACTS!

- Both Portsmouth and Norfolk are named for places in England.

- Baltimore was incorporated as a town in 1729. It didn't officially become a city until 1796.

- The "DC" in Washington, DC, stands for District of Columbia.

- In 1963, Virginia Beach and Princess Anne county joined together to become the City of Virginia Beach.

29

GLOSSARY

American Civil War: a war fought from 1861 to 1865 in the United States between the Union (the Northern states) and the Confederacy (the Southern states)

American Revolution: the war in which the colonies won their freedom from England (1775–1783)

conservation: the care of the natural world

ecosystem: all the living things in an area

habitat: the natural place where an animal or plant lives

humidity: the amount of water in the air

immigrant: one who comes to a new country to settle there

maritime: relating to the sea or sailing

peninsula: a narrow piece of land that extends into water from the mainland

tributary: a stream that flows into a larger body of water

unique: one of a kind

watershed: the whole area that drains into a body of water

FOR MORE INFORMATION

Books

Cunningham, Kevin. *The Virginia Colony.* New York, NY: Children's Press, 2012.

Lusted, Marcia Amidon. *Maryland: The Old Line State.* New York, NY: PowerKids Press, 2010.

Marsico, Katie. *The Chesapeake Bay.* Ann Arbor, MI: Cherry Lake Publishing, 2013.

Websites

Bay History
www.baygateways.net/history.cfm
Explore three timelines, which show settlement, growth, and information about the environment.

Chesapeake—Family Travel Guide
www.nationalgeographic.com/chesapeake/travel/
Start planning your trip to the Chesapeake Bay here!

Visit the Chesapeake
www.chesapeakebay.net/takeaction/visit
Use this website to find hiking trails, historic sites, and lots of other places to visit around the Chesapeake Bay.

INDEX